SAN FRANCISCO
On My Mind

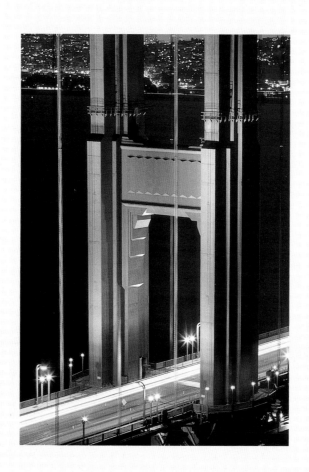

The
Globe
Pequot
Press

GUILFORD, CONNECTICUT

DAN HELLER

Project editor: David Singleton

Title page: Jon Gnass / Gnass Photo Images

Library of Congress Cataloging-in-Publication Data is available.
ISBN 0-7627-2519-2

Manufactured in the United States of America
First Edition/First Printing

City lights soaring to the sky,
Transamerica Pyramid DENNIS SHIRTCLIFF

An urban cascade in Golden Gate Park ALAN CHAPMAN

The main difficulty is getting to know her. She is not a big city, but her complexities are astounding. She is a maze of wonders and curiosities.

—T. H. WATKINS, *San Francisco in Color*

Clockwise from top left: Selling smells of all kinds; Willie Mays at Pacific Bell Park; advice for a sticky situation; Gandhi at the Embarcadero

Following pages: The Golden Gate Bridge and the city skyline rising above the clouds ED COOPER

A famous mile-and-a-half of U.S. Highway 101 heading to Marin County ED COOPER

DAN HELLER

INGER HOGSTROM

For the Gate is a big funnel, drawing in the winds and the mists which cool off the great, hot interior valleys of the San Joaquin and Sacramento. So the west wind blows steadily ten months of the year; and almost all the mornings are foggy.

—WILL IRWIN, *The City That Was*

It is an odd thing, but every one who disappears is said to be seen at San Francisco. It must be a delightful city, and possess all the attractions of the next world.

—OSCAR WILDE,
The Picture of Dorian Gray

FRANK S. BALTHIS

DAN HELLER

CHRISTIAN HEEB / GNASS PHOTO IMAGES

Rodin's "The Thinker"   INGER HOGSTROM

Mission Dolores Basilica   FRANK S. BALTHIS

Palace of Fine Arts   STEPHEN TRIMBLE

Saints Peter and Paul Church, North Beach
FRANK S. BALTHIS

San Francisco is one of the very few American cities to exude an attraction comparable to that of the venerable European capitols.

—T. H. WATKINS, *San Francisco in Color*

The rotunda at City Hall   DAN HELLER

City Hall   ED COOPER

Above and opposite: Views of a monument to the creative spirit, the Palace of Fine Arts, the Marina

San Francisco Opera House   DENNIS SHIRTCLIFF

San Francisco Museum of Modern Art

FRANK S. BALTHIS

Christopher Columbus below Coit Tower

CHRISTIAN HEEB / GNASS PHOTO IMAGES

California Palace of the Legion of Honor

CHRISTIAN HEEB / GNASS PHOTO IMAGES

Ventanta Temple

CHRISTIAN HEEB / GNASS PHOTO IMAGES

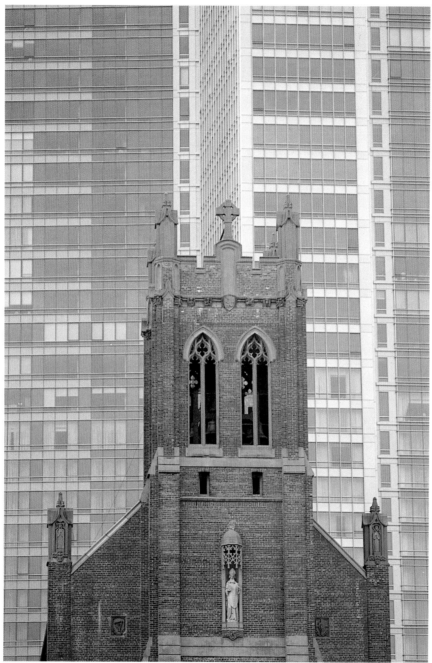

Holding its ground in a city of glass, Saint Patrick's Church, South of Market   Dan Heller

While the focus in the landscape of Old World cities was commonly government structures, churches, or the residences of rulers, the landscape and skyline of American cities have boasted their hotels, department stores, office buildings, apartments, and skyscrapers. In this grandeur, Americans have expressed their Booster Pride, their hopes for visitors and new settlers, and customers, for thriving commerce and industry.

—DANIEL J. BOORSTIN, *Democracy and Its Discontents: Reflections on Everyday Americans*

North Beach spires catching first light

Victorian sensibilities in a modern world, the Transamerica Pyramid and the Sentinel Building LARRY ULRICH

The Palace of Fine Arts lights up the Marina dusk. DAN HELLER

Turn up the lights; I don't want to go home in the dark.

—O. HENRY

All the lights say go on San Francisco's Broadway. DAN HELLER

No worries at this classic American diner DAN HELLER

Ghirardelli Square from the bay ED COOPER

A neighborhood experiencing two types of weather at once CHRISTIAN HEEB / GNASS PHOTO IMAGES

Yet the most characteristic thing after all was the coloring. The sea fog had a trick of painting every exposed object a sea gray which had a tinge of dull green in it. This, under the leaden sky of a San Francisco morning, had a depressing effect on first sight and afterward became a delight to the eye. For the color was soft, gentle and infinitely attractive in mass.

—WILL IRWIN, *The City That Was*

Looking up from Pier 39 as the clouds descend STEPHEN TRIMBLE

A wave of mist breaks over the San Francisco skyline. DAN HELLER

Painted ladies looking pretty on Alamo Square ED COOPER

Thousands of homeowners have transformed San Francisco into the most colorful city in the world. If there was a Nobel Prize for turning dead architecture into works of art, it would go to the homeowners, colorists, interior designers, and the craftspeople of San Francisco.

—ELIZABETH POMADA AND MICHAEL LARSON, *The Painted Ladies Revisited*

DAN HELLER

A Victorian beauty pageant, Alamo Square DAN HELLER

Parked on the edge in Nob Hill GEORGE WUERTHNER

When you get tired of walking around San Francisco,
you can always lean on it.

—LOCAL MAXIM

Taking the risk, descending Lombard Street   FRANK S. BALTHIS

Conservatory of Flowers, Golden Gate Park CHRISTIAN HEEB / GNASS PHOTO IMAGES

ROBIN MITCHELL

San Francisco is built on sand hills, but they are prolific sand hills. They yield a generous vegetation. All the rare flowers which people in "the States" rear with such patient care in parlor flower-pots and green-houses flourish luxuriantly in the open air there all year round. Calla lilies, all sorts of geraniums, passion flowers, moss roses—I do not know the names of a tenth part of them. I only know that while New Yorkers are burdened with banks and drifts of snow, Californians are burdened with banks and drifts of flowers, if they only keep their hands off and let them grow.

—MARK TWAIN, *Roughing It*

A gardener's dream of urban diversity, Strybing Arboretum, Golden Gate Park FRANK S. BALTHIS

Even downtown there's room for a meandering path, Yerba Buena Gardens. FRANK S. BALTHIS

Awake, O north wind, and come, O south wind!
Blow upon my garden that its fragrance may be
wafted abroad. Let my beloved come to his garden,
and eat its choicest fruits.

—*Song of Solomon 4:16*

Calm in a frantic city. Enjoying a respite in the Japanese
Tea Garden, Golden Gate Park DAN HELLER

Enlisted barracks along Fort Scott Walk, Presidio of San Francisco
FRANK S. BALTHIS

The service a man renders his friend is trivial and selfish, compared with the service he knows his friend stood in readiness to yield him, alike before he had begun to serve his friend, and now also. Compared with that good-will I bear my friend, the benefit it is in my power to render him seems small.

—RALPH WALDO EMERSON, "Gifts"

Flags wave for fallen heroes, San Francisco National Cemetery on Memorial Day. LAURENCE PARENT

DAN HELLER

ED COOPER

DAN HELLER

DAN HELLER

WILLIAM NEILL / LARRY ULRICH STOCK

DAN HELLER

DAN HELLER

The city is an urban kaleidoscope, shifting in color, mood and meaning from section to section, day to day, even hour to hour.

—T. H. WATKINS, *San Francisco in Color*

And if the city will never again enjoy the visibly unchecked opulence of the Bonanza Kings, their twentieth-century corporate equivalents have erected one concrete-and-glass monument after another, testifying to their own brand of superb self-satisfaction and creating a skyline of respectable impact.

—T. H. WATKINS, *San Francisco in Color*

Fire escapes with Chinese style STEPHEN TRIMBLE

Doing the day's shopping STEPHEN TRIMBLE

Here little China flaunts her scarlet streamers overhead, and flanks her doors with legends in saffron and gold; even its window-panes have a foreign look, and within is a glimmering of tinsel, a subdued light, and china lamps flickering . . . [the] air is laden with the fumes of smoking sandalwood . . .

—CHARLES WARREN STODDARD,
In the Footprints of the Padres

STEPHEN TRIMBLE

A busy street all the way up LOREN IRVING / GNASS PHOTO IMAGES

43

Heading downhill to Fisherman's Wharf DAN HELLER

To be where little cable cars climb halfway to the stars.

—DOUGLASS CROSS,
"I Left My Heart in San Francisco"

Rolling through downtown DAN HELLER

FRANK S. BALTHIS

A walking town, blessedly limited and cleansed by the bay and ocean, San Francisco is also America's last great metropolitan village. It is a place to be explained, like the blind man defining an elephant—different wherever you happen to touch it.

—HERBERT GOLD, *Travels in San Francisco*

FRANK S. BALTHIS

DAN HELLER

DAN HELLER

DAN HELLER

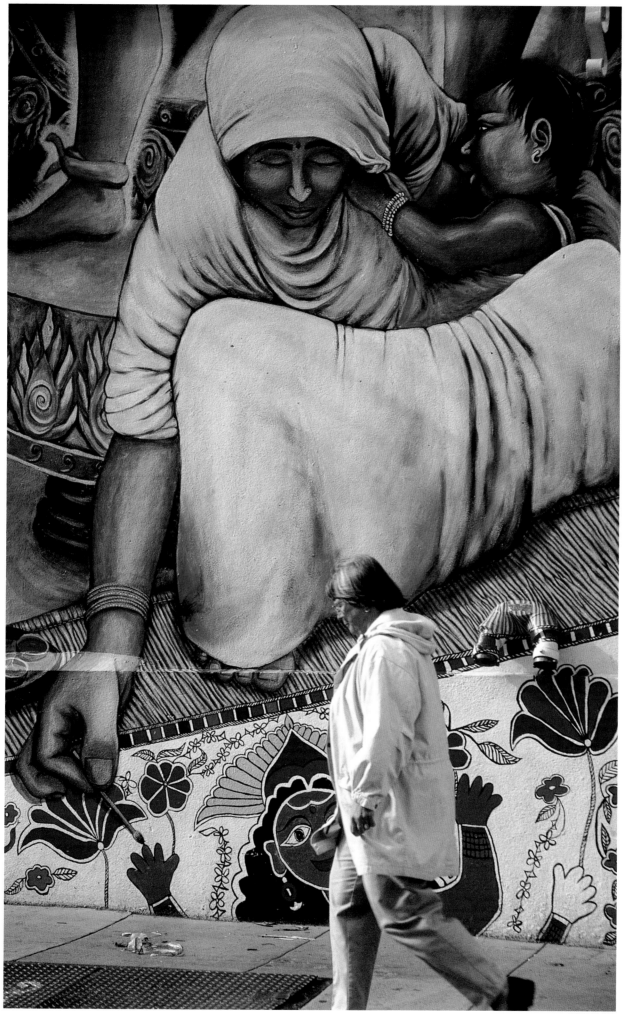

47

DAN HELLER

The bonny, merry city—the good, gray city . . . the gayest, lightest hearted, most pleasure loving city on the western continent . . .

—WILL IRWIN

DAN HELLER

DAN HELLER

DAN HELLER

Resident sea lions taking in the sun   LOREN IRVING / GNASS PHOTO IMAGES

Tour boats ready to embark   LOREN IRVING / GNASS PHOTO IMAGES

The girls taking a rest between outings, Hyde Street Pier LARRY ULRICH

A web of lines at the end of the day, Fisherman's Wharf ED COOPER

*If California ever becomes a prosperous country, this bay will be the
centre of its prosperity. The abundance of wood and water, the extreme
fertility of its shores, the excellence of its climate, which is as near to
being perfect as any in the world, and its facilities for navigation,
affording the best anchoring-grounds in the whole western coast of
America, all fit it for a place of great importance. . . .*

—RICHARD HENRY DANA, *Two Years Before the Mast*

Kite flying on Chrissy Field DAN HELLER

The wind is old and still at play
While I must hurry upon my way,
For I am running to Paradise;
Yet never have I lit on a friend
To take my fancy like the wind
That nobody can buy or bind. . . .

—WILLIAM BUTLER YEATS,
"Running to Paradise"

Resting on the pedals at Aquatic Park FRANK S. BALTHIS

Windsurfing off Candlestick Point FRANK S. BALTHIS

Alcatraz, the federal prison with a name like the blare of a trombone, [is] a black molar in the jawbone of the nation's prison system.

—THOMAS E. GADDIS, *Birdman of Alcatraz*

A different kind of cul-de-sac, China Beach DAN HELLER

Taking advantage of time and place DAN HELLER

Total physical and mental inertia are highly agreeable, much more so than we allow ourselves to imagine. A beach not only permits such inertia but enforces it, thus neatly eliminating all problems of guilt. It is now the only place in our overly active world that does.

—JOHN KENNETH GALBRAITH, Foreword to *The Beach Book* by Gloria Steinem

Three-dimensional views inside and out, Camera Obscura, Cliff House, Point Lobos FRANK S. BALTHIS

A few purple curves added, Candlestick Point State Recreation Area FRANK S. BALTHIS

Following pages: A carpet of fog filling the Bay Area's low spots DAN HELLER

A big first step over the Pacific DAN HELLER

Play with a view DAN HELLER

A ship heading to port CHRISTIAN HEEB / GNASS PHOTO IMAGES

The particular hill on which they were, out-jutted from the regular
line of the range, so that the sweep of their vision extended over
three-quarters of the circle. Below, on the flat land bordering the
bay, lay Oakland, and across the bay was San Francisco. Between
the two cities they could see the white ferry-boats on the water.

—JACK LONDON, *Burning Daylight*

The Bay Bridge at sunset FRANK S. BALTHIS

Crossing the eastern Bay Bridge between Oakland and Yerba Buena Island FRANK S. BALTHIS

The bay, or, as it was commonly called, the canal of Santa Barbara, is very large, being formed by the main land on one side, . . . and the whole swell of the Pacific Ocean rolls in here before a south-easter, and breaks with so heavy a surf in the shallow waters, that it is highly dangerous to lie near in to the shore during the south-easter season, that is, between the months of November and April.

—RICHARD HENRY DANA, *Two Years Before the Mast*

Seagulls swarming a fishing boat in the shadow of Alcatraz DAN HELLER

East Brother Island Light Station, Richmond PHILIP WRIGHT

Coming to Oakland Harbor on the Oakland–San Francisco Ferry TOM FELTS

Oakland Victorian, Ninth Street ROBIN MITCHELL

All that a city will ever allow you is an angle on it—an oblique, indirect sample of what it contains, or what passes through it; a point of view.

—PETER CONRAD

Federal Building, Oakland ROBIN MITCHELL

Seafaring craft new and old, Jack London
Waterfront, Oakland TOM FELTS

Quiet solitude in Inverness, Tomales Bay DENNIS SHIRTCLIFF

Strolling to Point Bonita, Golden Gate National Recreation Area GEORGE WUERTHNER

A rock rises like a whale's back on Stinson Beach, Golden Gate National Recreation Area. WILLIAM NEILL / LARRY ULRICH STOCK

Point Bonita Lighthouse guarding what Francis Drake missed in 1579, Golden Gate National Recreation Area   LAURENCE PARENT

Far off, blurred on the breast of the sea, can be seen the Farallones, which Sir Francis Drake passed on a S. W. course in the thick of what he describes as a "stynking fog." Well might he call it that, and a few other names, for it was the fog that robbed him of the glory of discovering San Francisco Bay.

—JACK LONDON, "Four Horses and a Sailor"

White cliffs at sunset along Drakes Beach, Point Reyes National Seashore INGER HOGSTROM

Beachcombers ambling along Ocean Beach, south of Point Lobos FRANK S. BALTHIS

A surfer gets his picture taken, Muir Beach, Golden Gate National Recreation Area.
INGER HOGSTROM

Following pages: Beginning a long night's work, Point
Montara Lighthouse LARRY CARVER

Water flowing through the verdant forest, Webb Creek, Mount Tamalpais State Park LARRY CARVER

Fog off Stinson Beach, below Mount Tamalpais

Tamalpais is a wooded mountain, with ample slopes, and from it on the north stretch away ridges of forest land, the outposts of the great Northern woods of Sequoia sempervirens. *This mountain and the mountainous country to the south bring the real forest closer to San Francisco than to any other American city.*

—WILL IRWIN, *The City That Was*

A path through the ancients, Muir Woods National Monument

Europe never had trees like the redwoods, whose life span number over two thousand years. This forest is the idea of forest, a prototype drawn by God; no church columns attain that height, and never does a church's semi-darkness contrast so sharply with a ray slanting in from above the reach of sight.

—CZESLAW MILOSZ, "Symbolic Mountains and Forests"

Soaring pillars of wood, Muir Woods National Monument

Fingers of fog rolling into Sausalito FRANK S. BALTHIS

I pointed out to him the great panorama spreading away to the horizon and four thousand feet beneath us. There lay San Francisco Bay like a great placid lake, the haze of smoke over the city, the Golden Gate, the ocean fog—rim beyond, and Mount Tamalpais over all, clear-cut and sharp against the sky.

—JACK LONDON, "An Adventure in the Upper Sea"

Mount Tamalpais rising 2,610 feet above the Sausalito marina ED COOPER

High grass in the early sun, Mount Tamalpais RICK SCHAFER

Marina masts reach for the city skyline. DAN HELLER

Market Street trolleys ready for the new day FRANK S. BALTHIS

THEY MADE IT POSSIBLE

San Francisco Trail on My Mind would have been impossible to produce without the creative and technical skills of the professional photographers who succeeded in a difficult task—capturing the many moods, people, buildings, and natural wonders in and around San Francisco.

From the the Golden Gate Bridge to the busy streets of Chinatown, San Francisco contains a breathtaking array of beautiful images, but transforming these images onto film requires more than just a camera. It takes an eye for composition, technical expertise, long hours of work, and the sheer determination to obtain a memorable shot rather than a mere snapshot.

The photographers who contributed to *San Francisco on My Mind* provided this extra skill and effort. They hiked, climbed, waited, and watched to get the best possible images from all parts of the Bay Area.

To all the excellent photographers who contributed to *San Francisco on My Mind,* thank you.

—THE GLOBE PEQUOT PRESS

Photographers in *San Francisco on My Mind*
Frank S. Balthis
Larry Carver
Alan Chapman
Ed Cooper
Terry Donnelly
Tom Felts
Jon Gnass
Christian Heeb
Dan Heller
Inger Hogstrom
Loren Irving
Robin Mitchell
William Neill
Laurence Parent
Rick Schafer
Dennis Shirtcliff
Scott T. Smith
Stephen Trimble
Larry Ulrich
Philip Wright
George Wuerthner

And these photo agencies:
Larry Ulrich Stock Photography, Inc.
Gnass Photo Images

SOURCE ACKNOWLEDGMENTS

The publisher gratefully acknowledges the following sources:

page 4, T. H. Watkins, *San Francisco in Color* (New York: Hastings House, Publishers, Inc., 1968), 20.

page 9, Will Irwin, *The City That Was; a requiem of old San Francisco* (Ubana Ill.: Project Gutenburg, 1906, reprinted 2002).

page 10, Oscar Wilde, *The Picture of Dorian Gray* from *Columbia World of Quotations*, ed. Robert Andrews, Mary Biggs, and Michael Seidel (New York: Columbia University Press, 1996), No. 64421.

page 13, Watkins, *San Francisco in Color*, 7.

page 19, Daniel J. Boorstin from *Democracy and Its Discontents: Reflections on Everyday Americans* (New York: Random House, 1974) from *Columbia World of Quotations*, No. 7779.

page 22, last words of William Sydney Porter from a 1907 song by Harry Williams quoted in *O. Henry* by Charles Alphonso Smith, from *Columbia World of Quotations*, No. 42756.

page 25, Irwin, *The City That Was*.

page 28, Elizabeth Pomada, Michael Larson, and Douglas Keister (photographer), *The Painted Ladies Revisited: San Francisco's Resplendent Victorians Inside and Out* (New York: E.P. Dutton, 1989), 9.

page 30, *Avant Guide San Francisco: Insiders' Guide for Cosmopolitan Travelers*, eds. Dan Levine and Michelle Goldberg (Studio City, Calif.: Empire Publishing Service, 2000).

page 32, Mark Twain, *Roughing It*, ed. and introduction by Hamlin Hill (New York: Viking Penguin Inc., 1981), 410.

page 34, *Song of Solomon* 4:16 from *Columbia World of Quotations*, No. 411.

page 38, Ralph Waldo Emerson from "Gifts" in *Essays, Second Series* (1844) from *Columbia World of Quotations*, No. 20118.

page 39, Watkins, *San Francisco in Color*, 22–23.

page 40, Ibid., 29.

page 43, Charles Warren Stoddard, *In the Footprints of the Padres* (San Francisco: A.M. Robertson, 1902).

page 45, Douglass Cross, "I Left My Heart in San Francisco" (General Music Publishing Co., 1962) from *Columbia World of Quotations*, No. 15445.

page 46, Herbert Gold, *Travels in San Francisco* (New York: Little, Brown and Company, 1990), 4.

page 48, Will Irwin quoted in T. H. Watkins, *San Francisco in Color*, 15.

page 53, Richard Henry Dana, *Two Years Before the Mast* (Boston: Houghton Mifflin, 1911).

page 55, William Butler Yeats, "Running to Paradise" from *Columbia World of Quotations*, No. 66157.

page 57, Thomas E. Gaddis, *Birdman of Alcatraz* (New York: Random House, 1955).

page 59, John Kenneth Galbraith, Forward to *The Beach Book* by Gloria Steinem from *Columbia World of Quotations*, No. 24301.

page 66, Jack London, *Burning Daylight* serialized in the *New York Herald*, June-August (1910).

page 69, Dana, *Two Years Before the Mast*.

page 72, Peter Conrad from an article in the *Independent on Sunday* (London: March 11, 1990) from *Columbia World of Quotations*, No. 13236.

page 77, Jack London, "Four Horses and a Sailor" in *The Human Drift* (New York: Macmillan, 1917).

page 85, Irwin, *The City That Was*.

page 86, Czeslaw Milosz, "Symbolic Mountains and Forests," *Visions from San Francisco Bay* (New York: Farrar, Straus & Giroux, 1982) from *Columbia World of Quotations*, No. 39817.

page 89, Jack London, "An Adventure in the Upper Sea" in *Dutch Courage and Other Stories* (New York: Macmillan, 1922).